agony of Apostrophes

Sylvia Fielding

First Edition (electronic): September 2013

Second Edition (print): May 2017

ISBN 978-1-5272-0815-5

Published by Warrina Books

"Sylvia has produced a fresh and succinct way of mastering the use of the apostrophe. I particularly liked her many references to the everyday use of language. I thoroughly recommend it as an invaluable reference for all those involved in learning and teaching."

Patrick Larkin BA H Dip Ed
Assistant Principal
Former Chairman of Teachers' Association of Media Education

My thanks go to my family, friends and colleagues for their encouragement and support, and to all my website visitors whose apostrophe queries provided the basis for this book.

Contents

Introduction

This book answers the questions:

- Do I need an apostrophe in this?
- If so, why, and where does it go?

I've named this book "The Agony of Apostrophes" because I know that many people do agonise over where to put an apostrophe. In fact, nothing seems to cause us more trouble in English grammar than the apostrophe—and it's not even easy to spell.

On my website www.commasense.co.uk I invite people to email me with their apostrophe queries. Even though the rules are on there, it's become clear to me that people need to see lots of examples in order to find or work out the answer to their own particular problem. The content of this book is based on those queries and I have attempted to explain and show the correct use of the apostrophe in the many real situations that have been posed to me.

I was shocked to receive an email from a mother whose daughter's English homework had been incorrectly 'corrected' by her school teacher. The mother wrote to me for confirmation that what her daughter had written was, in fact, correct. The daughter had written, "the dog gave its owner the ball" but the teacher had corrected it to "the dog gave it's owner the ball", meaning: "the dog gave

it is owner the ball", which is clearly nonsense. The only time an apostrophe should be inserted in the word "its" is when it is short for "it is" or "it has". The daughter's version, "the dog gave its owner the ball" is correct because the word "its" (without an apostrophe) is the equivalent of "his, her, our, my, your, their"—"its" is the version that means belonging to, or associated with, a thing or person/animal of unspecified gender.

Of course, even a teacher of English could be forgiven for making a mistake as a one-off, but apparently this wasn't the only correction he had made. The daughter had also written, "buy your cucumbers and lettuces here", which the teacher had corrected to "buy your cucumber's and lettuce's here". The teacher had inserted apostrophes into what are straightforward plural nouns, that is, "cucumbers and lettuces", which the daughter had written correctly.

Fortunately, I've always been able to "do" apostrophes but, in the process of writing this book, I've come to realise that apostrophes are not that simple; so I won't pretend they are.

If we didn't have to bother with apostrophes, writing would be so much easier but, for me, it would take all the enjoyment out of writing. Personally, I love the challenge of using apostrophes to make sense of what I'm trying to convey to the reader.

To illustrate how the apostrophe clarifies meaning, take a look at the following statements:

These are my brothers
these (people) are my brothers
These are my brother's
these (things) belong to my brother
These are my brothers'
these (things) belong to my brothers

In spoken language we can't see where the apostrophe is and, because we're usually face-to-face in conversation with someone, the meaning is clear in the context of what's being said. However, in written language the text can be ambiguous if the apostrophe is missing. In this sense, the apostrophe plays a useful and important role in making the meaning of written text clear.

There are several books containing rules on how to use the apostrophe, but my intention for this book is to communicate not only how to use it correctly and effectively, but also to create a reference book that is easy to use and which, hopefully, will become indispensable. How many times have you looked up a rule in a grammar book, or something in a dictionary, only to find that the example or guidance you're looking for isn't there and you're still none the wiser?

I've deliberately written this book with contractions (as in "I've" instead of "I have") to illustrate the broad use of the apostrophe, rather than the more formal way of keeping contractions in written text to a minimum.

And I've agonised over trying to come up with simple ways to explain where an apostrophe should go – I hope I've achieved this.

This is the second edition of my book in that it has an Appendix containing a sample of real apostrophe queries that have been emailed to me via my website since writing the first edition. The queries are in question and answer format, albeit with names changed where appropriate. I hope that other people's queries might provide the answers you may be looking for.

The first edition was in e-book format, but I soon realised that e-books do not work well as reference books. Finding the necessary information is nowhere near as easy as looking for answers in a physical book, which is why I decided to publish a paperback version.

If, after referring to this book, you still have unanswered questions or queries about how to use the apostrophe, feel free to email me at:

sfielding@commasense.co.uk

In this book, you will find the answers to questions such as:

- Why do I need an apostrophe?
- What are the rules for using apostrophes?
- When should I put an apostrophe in *its*?
- Do I need an apostrophe in *peoples*?
- Where does the apostrophe go in *childrens*?
- How do I make a word possessive?
- Should I put the "s" before or after my apostrophe?
- How do I treat words ending in "s"?
- Where do I put the apostrophe in someone's name?
- Should it be *Thomas's* car or *Thomas'* car?
- Do I need an apostrophe in *phone* or *pub*?
- Should *theirs* or *ours* have an apostrophe?
- Is it *your welcome* or *you're welcome*?
- Should it be *MOTs* or *MOT's*?
- Is it *potato's* or *potatoes*?
- Do abbreviations need an apostrophe?

So, why not begin by testing your knowledge of apostrophes using the quiz on the next page? Everything in the quiz, and more, is covered in the chapters of this book. There are 30 questions in total, and the answers can be found at the end of the book. (Note, you will need to jot down the numbers for your chosen answers.)

Introductory apostrophe quiz

1a) The peoples' vote
1b) The people's vote

2a) Is this mine or yours?
2b) Is this mine or your's?

3a) The man, whose car I crashed into, is my neighbour
3b) The man, who's car I crashed into, is my neighbour

4a) Jack is a friend of my mother
4b) Jack is a friend of my mother's

5a) The boy's were told the sweets were all their's
5b) The boys were told the sweets were all theirs
5c) The boys were told the sweets were all their's
5d) The boy's were told the sweets were all theirs

6a) Two weeks notice
6b) Two weeks' notice
6c) Two week's notice

7a) The men's wives went with them on the trip
7b) The mens' wives went with them on the trip

8a) Where are the womens' toilets?
8b) Where are the women's toilets?

9a) Who told you its yours?
9b) Who told you it's yours?
9c) Who told you its your's?
9d) Who told you it's your's?

10a) Who's that man?
10b) Whose that man?

11a) Mr and Mrs Smith's house was burgled
11b) Mr and Mrs Smiths' house was burgled

12a) The Smiths' house is in darkness
12b) The Smith's house is in darkness

13a) MOTs carried out here
13b) MOT's carried out here

14a) Whose bag is this?
14b) Who's bag is this?

15a) Mind your P's and Q's
15b) Mind your Ps and Qs

16a) The salad contained lettuces and tomatoes
16b) The salad contained lettuce's and tomato's

17a) Which shoes? The red or the white one's?
17b) Which shoes? The red or the white ones?

18a) Your late!
18b) You're late!

19a) The dog has injured it's paw
19b) The dog has injured its paw

20a) Shall we go to the children's playground?
20b) Shall we go to the childrens' playground?

21a) I've been invited to Sue and Mark's wedding
21b) I've been invited to Sue's and Mark's wedding

22a) Don't forget your phone
22b) Don't forget your 'phone

23a) She was born in the '20s
23b) She was born in the 20's

24a) He was born in the 1920's
24b) He was born in the 1920s

25a) Look where you're going!
25b) Look where your going!

26a) The rain’s stopped
26b) The rains stopped

27a) Policemen’s helmets
27b) Policemens’ helmets

28a) Tell me it’s not going to rain
28b) Tell me its not going to rain

29a) The company has expanded its product portfolio
29b) The company has expanded it’s product portfolio

30a) Women’s shoes are next to the ladies’ handbags
30b) Womens’ shoes are next to the ladies’ handbags

Please go to the **Answers to quizzes** chapter at the end of the book for the correct answers. There you will also find the relevant chapter references which will allow you to look up the rules or theory associated with each correct answer.

1 – Using the apostrophe to show possession

(How to show that something belongs to someone or something)

If you have trouble knowing where to put an apostrophe, you are certainly not alone. In fact, nothing seems to cause more trouble in English grammar than the apostrophe. But if you follow the rules in this and subsequent chapters, you should be able to solve almost any apostrophe problem that crops up.

The apostrophe is mainly used to show possession—ownership of something—for example, *the girl's school bag*, or *the old people's care home*.

The French language uses a more formal and long-winded way of showing possession, for example: *la mère de Marie* (the mother of Marie) or *le père de Jean* (the father of Jean). In the English language we rarely use this form; instead we would say *Marie's mother* and *Jean's father* although we mean *the mother of Marie* and *the father of Jean*. Likewise, we would not say *the school bag of the girl* or *the care home of the old people* as these phrases sound clumsy and too formal.

We also use the shortened form for phrases such as:

- two weeks' notice (notice of two weeks)
- one week's pay (pay of one week)
- one day's leave (leave of one day)

In the following phrases, the apostrophes have been deliberately omitted.

- The childs toys
- The students books
- The peoples vote
- The chickens eggs
- The childrens party

Written as they are, two of the above phrases are ambiguous – *the students books* could mean the books of one student or several students; similarly, *the chickens eggs* could be referring to one chicken or a few chickens, which is why we need an apostrophe to clarify the meaning. The other three phrases aren't ambiguous but they are incorrect without their apostrophes. So how do we work out where the apostrophes should go?

Below I will outline three different ways of working out where to put the apostrophe—each of the rules will work—it doesn't matter which you use, but you may wish to use all three to check that you've worked it out correctly.

The most commonly cited rule is to add ***'s*** to the end of singular words and also to plural words that do not end in an "s" (eg children, men, women, people). For plurals that end in an "s" (eg boys, ladies) just add an apostrophe to the end of the word after the "s".

However, here is an alternative rule that some may find useful:

To work out where the apostrophe should go, try changing the phrase or sentence around to its longer, more formal format containing the word "of". The apostrophe goes immediately after the last letter of the word or phrase that follows the word "of".

Here are the phrases written in their longer form and in their shorter form using the apostrophe correctly:

- The toys of **the child** = **the child**'s toys
- The books of **the students = the students**' books
- The vote of **the people = the people**'s vote
- The eggs of **the chicken = the chicken**'s eggs

- The party of **the children = the children**'s party

In the following examples, the rule works in the same way:

- Notice of **two weeks = two weeks'** notice
- Pay of **one week = one week's** pay
- Leave of **one day = one day's** leave
- The bag of **Cheryl = Cheryl's** bag
- The laptop of **Mike = Mike's** laptop

> Yet another way of determining where the apostrophe should go is to ask the following question: *To whom or to what does it belong or refer?* The apostrophe then goes immediately after whatever word is the answer to that question.

Again, the apostrophes in the following phrases have been omitted.

1. The childs toys
2. The students books (*several students*)
3. The peoples vote
4. The chickens eggs (*one chicken*)
5. The childrens Christmas party

To determine where the apostrophes should go, the questions to ask are:

1. Who do the toys belong to? The answer is the **child** - the apostrophe goes immediately after the word "child" before the 's'. The correct statement is: The child's toys.
2. Who do the books belong to? The answer is the **students** - the apostrophe goes immediately after the word "students", after the 's'. The correct statement is: The students' books. (Note: if the book belonged to one student, the apostrophe would go after the word *student* and would be written: The student's books.)
3. Who does the vote belong to? The answer is the **people** - the apostrophe goes immediately after the word "people" before the "s". The correct statement is: The people's vote. (Note that *people* is already a plural word and to write *peoples'* would be incorrect.)
4. Who do the eggs belong to? The answer is the **chicken** - the apostrophe goes immediately after the word "chicken" before the 's'. The correct statement is: The chicken's eggs. (Note: if the eggs belonged to several chickens, the apostrophe would go after the word *chickens* and would be written: The chickens' eggs.)
5. Who does the Christmas party belong to? (Who is the Christmas party for?) The answer is the **children** - the apostrophe goes immediately after the word "children" before the 's'. The correct statement is: The children's Christmas party. (Note that *children* is already

a plural word and to write *childrens'* would be incorrect.)

2 – Contractions and abbreviations

(Using apostrophes with shortened words)

The apostrophe is also used to show that a letter, or letters, are missing from a word. A *contraction* is when two words have been contracted into one word, for example, *I've* (I have), *haven't* (have not), *isn't* (is not), *you'll* (you will *or* you shall), *it's* (it is). Contractions must have apostrophes to show where the missing letters are. An *abbreviation* is where a single word has been shortened, for example, pub, phone, demo – abbreviations do not need apostrophes.

Contractions

Where've you put the letter? *(Where have you put the letter?)*
Where's it gone? *(Where has it gone?)*
Where's Cindy? *(Where is Cindy?)*
What've you done? *(What have you done?)*
Who's there? *(Who is there?)*
Who's been a good boy? *(Who has been a good boy?)*
Note: don't confuse "who's" meaning "who is" with "whose" (see chapter 9)
Let's go *(Let us go)*
Why's that? *(Why is that?)*
You're welcome *(You are welcome)*
Note: a common mistake is to write "your welcome"

Don't do that *(Do not do that)*
She'd prefer not to go *(She would prefer not to go)*
When I arrived, she'd gone *(When I arrived, she had gone)*
I'll have to admit I'm sorry *(I will/shall have to admit I am sorry)*
We'll definitely be there *(We will definitely be there)*
I'm hungry *(I am hungry)*
I didn't see you there *(I did not see you there)*
Mandy's off to Glastonbury *(Mandy is off to Glastonbury)*
Geoff isn't coming *(Geoff is not coming)*
The alarm hasn't gone off yet *(The alarm has not gone off yet)*
We're almost there *(We are almost there)*
Why's it important? *(Why is it important?)*
What's that? *(What is that?)*
What's he been doing? *(What has he been doing?)*
They're also suffering *(They are also suffering)*
Note: don't confuse "they're" with "their" (see chapter 10)
9 o'clock *(9 of the clock—no longer in use in today's English)*
Anywhere that's blue on the map shows where we've been flooded
(Anywhere that is blue on the map shows where we have been flooded)

As you're studying science at school you'll know the answers
(As you are studying science at school you will know the answers)
Note: to write "As your studying science..." is incorrect
It's going to feel bitterly cold *(It is going to feel bitterly cold)*
It isn't the right address *(It is not the right address)*
Here's your bus *(Here is your bus)*
Most people who aren't scientists wouldn't understand
(Most people who are not scientists would not understand)
The sky's the limit *(The sky is the limit)*
My keys aren't there *(My keys are not there)*
He won't stop staring *(He will not stop staring)*
Note: "won't" is the abbreviated form of "will not"—strange as it seems; and "shan't is the abbreviated form of "shall not"
I shan't be coming with you *(I shall not be coming with you)*
I shouldn't think so *(I should not think so)*

Abbreviations

Where a word has simply been abbreviated (a clipped word), for example, *ad, advert, pub, demo, flu, phone*, it does not require an apostrophe and to insert one would be incorrect.

- She’s got the flu.
- Are you going to the pub?
- Where’s my phone?
- I love that advert (or, I love that ad).
- Would you like to see a demo of that?

However, apostrophes <u>are</u> needed in colloquial dialects (where the abbreviation is not a formally accepted word):

- Are you comin’ with me or goin’ with him?

And in terms such as:

- Fish ‘n’ chips
- Pick ‘n’ mix
- Born in ’73
- The ‘90s; the ‘80s

Note: when referring to something that happened in, say, the 1920s this does not take an apostrophe but when abbreviating it to the ‘90s then it needs an apostrophe. There is no apostrophe needed before the “s”, however.

3 – Its or It's?

(When to use *Its* and when to use *It's*)

Many of us are confused about whether to use *its* or *it's* and getting it wrong can be embarrassing both for the writer and the reader. But if you follow this simple rule, I guarantee you will never get it wrong again.

The only time you need an apostrophe in *its* is when it is short for *it is* or *it has*.

When being used in a possessive sense, for example, *the dog has lost* ***its*** *bone*, this should never have an apostrophe. If an apostrophe is inserted, the sentence is then saying, "The dog has lost *it is* (or *it has*) bone", which is clearly wrong. So, *its* without an apostrophe is always possessive and means belonging to something; it is the equivalent of *my, his, her, our, your and their,* when the gender is unknown or it is a 'thing', for example, *I need a new calculator – its keys keep sticking*.

Here's a paragraph showing the correct use of *its* and *it's*:

There's a lot of disagreement over whether it's wise to wash our hair every day. Some say that the hair on our heads should be washed as frequently as we take a bath or shower. Others say that shampoo, with its harsh chemicals, dries out the hair too much and that it's best to leave hair for several days between washes. Whether it's good for us or not to wash hair daily, it's been proven that hair will eventually cleanse itself through its own natural oils when left for long periods of time; its ability to self-clean has been well researched. It's a controversial subject but it's all down to personal preference in the end.

All the instances of *it's* in the above paragraph can be substituted either for *it is* or *it has*, that is, they are short for *it is* or *it has*. All the instances of *its* are possessive. Try substituting *it is* or *it has* in their places and the passage will not make sense. This is the test you can apply every time you use *its* or *it's.* If it has an apostrophe it can only mean *it is* or *it has.*

As a further example, the following is correct:

It's obvious that its mother has abandoned it (referring to a lost kitten, gender unknown).

Now try testing yourself on the use of *its* and *it’s* – which of the following is the correct version?

1. a) It's time to go!
   b) Its time to go!

2. a) The dog’s eaten its lunch
   b) The dog’s eaten it's lunch

3. a) Let's not forget that its only been a year
   b) Let's not forget that it's only been a year

4. a) Its my job to safeguard its location
   b) Its my job to safeguard it's location
   c) It's my job to safeguard it's location
   d) It's my job to safeguard its location

5. a) The project team achieved all of its deliverables
   b) The project team achieved all of it's deliverables

6. a) Unfortunately it's been taken out of my hands
   b) Unfortunately its been taken out of my hands

7. a) If its genuine, where’s its label?
   b) If it's genuine, where’s its label?
   c) If it's genuine, where’s it's label?
   d) If its genuine, where’s it's label?

8. a) It's already been useful; it's worth its weight in gold
   b) It's already been useful; its worth its weight in gold
   c) Its already been useful; it's worth it's weight in gold
   d) It's already been useful; it's worth it's weight in gold
   e) Its already been useful; its worth it's weight in gold
   f) Its already been useful; its worth its weight in gold

9. a) Poor baby—it's crying because it's dropped it's toy
   b) Poor baby—its crying because its dropped its toy
   c) Poor baby—it's crying because it's dropped its toy
   d) Poor baby—it's crying because its dropped it's toy
   e) Poor baby—its crying because it's dropped it's toy
   f) Poor baby—it's crying because its dropped its toy

Please go to the **Answers to Quizzes** chapter at the end of the book for the correct answers.

4 – Making plural words possessive

(How to use an apostrophe to show that something belongs to more than one thing or person)

This is also covered in chapter 1 but, as plurals can sometimes be trickier, this section contains examples of how to use the possessive apostrophe with plural nouns that end with an "s" and the few that do not end in an "s".

Here's a reminder of the rule: add ***'s*** to the end of plural words that do not end in an "s" (eg children, men, women, people), but for plurals that end in an "s" (which is the majority, eg ladies, friends) just add an apostrophe to the end of the word after the "s".

The apostrophe used correctly with plural words that do not end in "s":

- Men's fashion
- Children's books
- The children's playground
- People's preferences
- The people's choice
- The mice's cage
- Men's captain
- Men's hats
- Women's toilets (but ladies' toilets)

The apostrophe used correctly with plural words ending in "s":

- Babies' clothes
- Ladies' tennis tournament
- Ladies' fashions
- Seniors' captain
- Members' award evening
- The athletes' changing room
- The libraries' fate
- The twins' birthday

Note: it doesn't matter whether there are one or several *books* or *choices* or *preferences* or *tournaments*—it doesn't change the position of the apostrophe, ie

- children's books are over there
- my favourite children's book

Remember – if the plural ends in "s", put the apostrophe after it; if it doesn't end in "s", add an apostrophe and an "s" to the end of the word.

5 – Apostrophe mistakes

(Errors seen in print and on public display)

Chiselborough is one of the areas' most sought-after villages. X
Chiselborough is one of the area's most sought-after villages. √

[If we change the sentence around, it would be *Chiselborough is one of the most sought-after villages of the area*. There is only one area and the apostrophe goes immediately after the word area before the "s".]

... with it's new one piece stainless steel door... X
... with its new one piece stainless steel door... √

[The first phrase is saying, "with **it is** new one piece stainless steel door"; the same mistake can be seen in the examples below.]

The car it's self is in good condition for its age. X
The car itself is in good condition for its age. √

This car has just been through it's MOT. X
This car has just been through its MOT. √

Gone are the days where school's required women to take sewing classes. X
Gone are the days where schools required women to take sewing classes.√

[In the above, an apostrophe should never be inserted in a straight plural; this sentence is not possessive.]

Seen in an official letter from the Royal Mail:
Dear Sir/Madam, I am writing to ask if you require your post to be delivered on Saturday's. X
Dear Sir/Madam, I am writing to ask if you require your post to be delivered on Saturdays. √

[Again, straight plurals do not need an apostrophe.]

On a well-known insurance company's website:
Almost 25 year's experience in providing health insurance X
Almost 25 years' experience in providing health insurance √

[This is referring to 25 years of experience and is therefore possessive—the experience refers to 25 years, not 25 year; the apostrophe should go after the "s" of years.] Note: "company's website" is correct because there is only one company – "companies' website" would be incorrect.

Exclusively for the over 50's X
Exclusively for the over 50s √

[no apostrophe needed—this is just a straight plural]

On a courier's website:
Your item is automatically covered up to it's full value. X
Your item is automatically covered up to its full value. √

[The first sentence is saying: Your item is automatically covered up to **it is** full value; the same mistake is shown in the examples below.]

On an estate agent's website:
Marketed for sale with the benefit of it's own private entrance. X
Marketed for sale with the benefit of its own private entrance. √

Seen in large print on a banner outside a new housing estate:
"We could buy your home for it's market value." X
"We could buy your home for its market value." √

On a health website:
"Known for it's healing powers, aloe vera..." X
"Known for its healing powers, aloe vera..."√

On a mobile broadband comparison website:
It's good to see a provider that is not over egging what they are selling and is big on treating its <u>customers'</u> fairly. X
It's good to see a provider that is not over egging what they are selling and is big on treating its <u>customers</u> fairly. √

[They have used the apostrophe correctly in both instances of *its* and *it's* but have wrongly inserted an apostrophe in a straight plural.]

6 – Ordinary plurals

(When <u>not</u> to use an apostrophe)

Ordinary plurals (ie referring to more than one of something) should never have apostrophes. Inserting an apostrophe into words such as *tomatoes, potatoes, cucumbers and lettuces* is known, albeit disrespectfully, as the Greengrocer's Apostrophe. I suspect many of us have seen "tomato's and potato's or even "tomatoe's and potatoe's" outside a Greengrocer's shop, but this is always incorrect when referring to more than one of something. Do not use an apostrophe to make something into a plural. The following plurals are correct.

- One tomato; two tomatoes
- One potato; two potatoes
- One day; two days
- One baby; two babies
- One lady; two ladies
- One MOT; two MOTs
- One CD; two CDs
- One DVD; two DVDs

There is one exception to this rule, which is when you're writing, for instance, "Mind your p's and q's". If you were to write, "mind your ps and qs", this would be confusing for the reader, which is why it's necessary to insert an apostrophe to clarify the meaning. However, if you were to write "mind your Ps and Qs", using upper case, then apostrophes aren't needed.

While we're on the subject of plurals, how do we make proper names, for example surnames, into plurals?

When a surname ends in an "s" simply add "es" to make it plural; when a surname does not end in an "s", simply add "s" to make it plural.

Mr and Mrs Thomas could be referred to as ***the Thomases***
Mr and Mrs Jones as ***the Joneses***
Mr and Mrs Lewis as ***the Lewises***
Mr and Mrs Smith as ***the Smiths***
Mr and Mrs Fielding as ***the Fieldings***
Mr and Mrs Dennis as ***the Dennises***
Mr and Mrs Phillips as ***the Phillipses***
Mr and Mrs Morris as ***the Morrises***

Again, do not add an apostrophe simply to make a name into a plural as in, for example, "I saw the Fielding's in town today"—this is incorrect—it should be written as "I saw the Fieldings in town today".

7 – Making names possessive

(How to use apostrophes with names)

Names do seem to cause a lot of problems; here are a few common surnames:

- Thomas
- Lewis
- Jones
- Smith
- Fielding
- Dennis
- Phillips
- Morris

Let's take the example of a house belonging to Mr Thomas, Lewis, etc; this is the correct way to write the phrases:

- Mr Thomas's house (the house of Mr Thomas)
- Mr Lewis's house (the house of Mr Lewis)
- Mr Jones's house (the house of Mr Jones)
- Mr Smith's house (the house of Mr Smith)
- Mr Fielding's house (the house of Mr Fielding)
- Mr Dennis's house (the house of Mr Dennis)
- Mr Phillips's house (the house of Mr Phillips)
- Mr Morris's house (the house of Mr Morris)

We simply add an **'s** to the name to show possession.

> Add **'s** to singular words and to plural words that do not end in an "s". For plural words ending in "s" just add an apostrophe after the "s".

or

> To determine where the apostrophe should go, change the phrase or sentence around to its longer, more formal format containing the word "of". The apostrophe goes immediately after the last letter of the word or phrase that follows the word "of".

So how do we write about a house belonging to the Thomases, the Lewises, etc? This is the correct way to write the phrases:

- The Thomases' house (the house of ***the Thomases***)
- The Lewises' house (the house of ***the Lewises***)
- The Joneses' house (the house of ***the Joneses***)
- The Smiths' house (the house of ***the Smiths***)
- The Fieldings' house (the house of ***the Fieldings***)

- The Dennises' house (the house of ***the Dennises***)
- The Phillipses' house (the house of ***the Phillipses***)
- The Morrises' house (the house of **the Morrises**)

However, when talking about a *household* we would simply use the family surname because the name in this instance is just describing the household (see chapter 8):

- The Thomas household
- The Lewis household
- The Jones household
- The Smith household
- The Fielding household
- The Dennis household
- The Phillips household
- The Brown household
- The Harris household
- The Morris household

While we're specifically looking at names, here are some more possessive examples – this time using first names:

- James's laptop (the laptop of James)
- St James's Square (the Square of St James)
- Marcus's address (the address of Marcus)
- Dennis's shirt (the shirt of Dennis)
- Chris's shoes (the shoes of Chris)

- Jess's children (the children of Jess)
- Charles's newspaper (the newspaper of Charles)
- Giles's sister (the sister of Giles)

There is one exception to adding **'s** to singular names, however (sorry, there's always an exception), and this is when the original name ends in an "iz" sound:

- Mercedes' trombone (girl's name Mercedes)
- The Mercedes' tyres
- Mrs Hodges' dog
- Mr Bridges' daughter

When talking about something belonging to a couple, for example *Jane and Simon*, the couple should be treated as if they were one entity with the apostrophe inserted after the last name.

- Jane and Simon's wedding
- Jack and Jill's pail of water
- Mum and Dad's anniversary
- Seb and Millie's parents
- Mr and Mrs Clark's daughter
- Mr and Mrs Evans's house

But, *Mr and Mrs Hodges' dog* and *Mr and Mrs Bridges' daughter* (see previous explanation above regarding names ending in an "iz" sound).

However, when the subject refers to two people or groups that are not linked and are separate, then an apostrophe would be needed in both:

- Where are the men's and women's clothing departments?
- Where are Sebastian's and Emilia's coats?

But what if we were talking about something belonging to me and my sister?

- My sister's and my views differed on the matter
- David's and her mother was always knitting

Admittedly, these last two sentences do sound odd, but they are correct. If writing these feels uncomfortable, use instead something like "Our views differed on the matter" and "their mother was always knitting" – provided of course that it's clear whom "our" and "their" are referring to.

8 – Possessive or adjective?

(Is it just a describing word—adjective—or does it need an apostrophe?)

(And words ending in "z")

So how should we treat words that end in "z", such as Heinz or Allianz?

If we were to talk about the customers of these organisations, it would be "Heinz's customers" and "Allianz's customers"—we simply add ***'s*** to make it possessive.

However, when we see 'Heinz Baked Beans' on a can, this doesn't in fact require an apostrophe because this is simply describing the type or brand of the baked beans. In the same way, I might describe myself as a Waitrose customer or a Tesco customer and, again, this does not need an apostrophe; I am simply describing the type or brand of customer that I am and, in these instances, the words *Waitrose* and *Tesco* are simply adjectives. If, however, we wanted to talk about the customers of Tesco or Waitrose then it would be Waitrose's customers and Tesco's customers. The difference is subtle. When something is merely an adjective, that is, describing something rather than belonging to or referring to something, then an apostrophe is not necessary.

Here are some examples:

Sports club
(describing the type of club, as in golf club and tennis club, for example)
Christmas lights
(describing the type of lights, rather than the lights of Christmas)
Library books
(describing the books, rather than books that belong to the library; if we were to write The Library's books, then this would mean the books belonging to the Library)
London Writers Group
(describing the type of group, ie a group in London for Writers; however it would not be incorrect to insert an apostrophe after "Writers" making it London Writers' Group which would then mean that it is a group of, or belonging to, the London writers)
Accounts department
(describing the department)
Pilates mat
(describing the type of mat used for Pilates)
Massed bands concert
(describing the type of concert)
Garden implements sale
(although this could be argued as a sale of garden implements, the apostrophe would not be wrong but it is also just describing the type of sale and therefore no apostrophe is necessary)

But what about something like *kids parties*? This is a slightly tricky one in that it could be argued that *kids* in this example could be an adjective describing the type of parties. If the word *kids* were substituted with, say, *childrens, womens, mens*, these clearly need an apostrophe as in *children's shoes, women's shoes or men's shoes*. The apostrophe could arguably be omitted in *kids parties*, but it may simply look as if someone has forgotten to put it in. My personal opinion is that *kids' parties* should be written with an apostrophe.

Here are examples both of when an apostrophe is needed and is not needed:

- The lawn was strewn with rose petals (describing the type of petals that were strewn over the lawn)
- The lawn was strewn with the rose's petals (meaning the lawn was strewn with petals belonging to a particular rose)
- The lawn was strewn with the roses' petals (meaning the lawn was strewn with the petals of several particular roses)
- Golf Superintendent's Newsletter
- Easter Newsletter

Lastly, company names are slightly tricky. Companies will often use apostrophes in their names according to their preference rather than according to any grammatical rule. We should therefore accept whichever convention is used or chosen by an organisation with regard to their trading names, for example, Waterstones, Barclays, Sainsbury’s.

9 – Whose or Who's?

(When to use Whose and when to use Who's)

Who's means either *who is* or *who has* and should never be used in the following way:

"Who's coat is this?" Written in this way, it's actually saying, "Who is coat is this?" or "Who has coat is this?" which is nonsense. The correct way to write this is "Whose coat is this?" ***Whose*** is a word meaning "of which, of whom". A few examples are:

- Whose house is this?
- Whose coat is red?
- Whose keys are these?
- The man whose car I crashed into is suing me.
- The book whose pages are torn is not worth keeping.
- The petrol station whose lights are off is closed.

If we substitute *whose* with *who's* the above sentences would be translated as:

- Who is house is this?
- Who is coat is this?
- Who is keys are these?
- The man who is car I crashed into is suing me.

- The book who is pages are torn is not worth keeping
- The petrol station who is lights are off is closed.

These do not make sense at all and *who's* would be incorrect in the above. So, whenever you use *who's* in a phrase or sentence, remember that it is short for *who is* or *who has* and if the sentence or phrase does not make sense using the longer version of *who's* then you need *whose* instead.

Some examples of the use of "who's":

- Who's got the tickets? *(Who has got the tickets?)*
- Who's he? *(Who is he?)*
- Who's there? *(Who is there?)*
- The woman who's looking in the shop window is my aunt *(The woman who is looking...)*
- Who's who in the world of fashion? *(Who is who...)*

Now some correct examples using both forms:

- Who's the man whose children are misbehaving?
  Who is the man whose children are misbehaving?

- Who's the woman who's lost her purse?
  Who is the woman who has lost her purse?

- Who's the guy who's looking annoyed?
  Who is the guy who is looking annoyed?

- Whose glasses are these? Who's lost their glasses?
  Whose glasses are these? Who has lost their glasses?

- Who's the man whose children's names are Ben and Megan?
  Who is the man whose children's names are Ben and Megan?

10 – Possessive adjectives & pronouns

(My, her, his, its, our, your, their, and mine, hers, his, its, ours, yours, theirs)

Possessive *adjectives* are words such as *my, her, his, its, our, your and their,* as in the following examples:

- My book
- Her car
- His coat
- Its owner
- Our house
- Your opinion
- Their fault

Possessive *pronouns* are what we would say in response to the question "Whose is this?" for example:

- Mine
- Hers
- His
- Its
- Ours
- Yours
- Theirs

None of the above should have an apostrophe but, unfortunately, we often see written *her's, our's, your's and their's,* but these are entirely incorrect.

And of course, as already mentioned in chapter 3, "it's" would also be wrong in this context.

11 – Examples with the apostrophe used correctly

(Lots of correct examples)

P = apostrophe used to denote possession
C = apostrophe used to denote missing letters (contraction)

This is our first full **year's** report as a Trust. (*P*)
It was a study on how to explore **one's** culture and the influences it has on routines
(ie the culture belonging to one) (*P*)
His **Master's** Voice (*P*)
The **Duke of Edinburgh's** role (*P*)
The **Prince of Wales's** visit (*P*)
My **sister-in-law's** birthday (*P*)
My **sisters-in-law's** wedding outfits were lovely (*P*)
(*Note: the plural of sister-in-law is sisters-in-law which is then treated, for example, like the word children, ie the children's outfits were lovely.)*
Maggie's pies (*P*)
Elvis's song (*P*)
It's just **people's** curiosity. (*C*, *P*)
Everyone's view is important to us. (*P*)
Something to suit **everyone's** taste. (*P*)
(Note that "everyone" is a singular word meaning "every one person")
Someone else's responsibility (*P*)

There's Annie **who's** a mother figure to them (*C*, *C*)
The **company's** mission statement (*P*)
A meeting of several finance **companies'** directors took place in London. (*P*)
A meeting of the finance **company's** directors took place in London (one company). (*P*)
The **child's** parents (*P*)
The **school's** reputation (*P*)
The child lost its way; **it's** easily done. (*C*)
The **men's** clothing shop (*P*)
The **men's** cars (*P*)
The **man's** children (*P*)
The **gentleman's** briefcase (*P*)
The **gentlemen's** bar (*P*)
Straight plurals **don't** have apostrophes. (*C*)
I am taking my **client's** instructions (one client). (*P*)
I am taking my **clients'** instructions (more than one client). (*P*)
The **boss's** office (*P*)
Mr **Cross's** salary (*P*)
Steve and Carol's party (*P*)
The **palace's** interior walls were covered with paintings. (*P*)
When **it's** gone, **it's** gone. (*C*, *C*)
Mrs **Ambrose's** dahlias (*P*)
Samuel **Pepys's** Diary (*P*)
A **joke's** a joke. (*C*)
Enough's enough. (*C*)
Whose are they? **They're** theirs. (*C*)

Who's the owner of these keys? (*C*)
Where's its label? (*C*)
Here's your book? **Where's** mine? **Where's** hers? (*C, C, C*)
The **ladies'** bags (*P*)
The **lady's** bags (*P*)
Buying this product helps save the **world's** forests. (*P*)
She was worried by her **father's** unhappiness. (*P*)
It's Angela's worst nightmare, **isn't** it? (*C, P, C*)
Jack has seven **years'** experience in design work. (*P*)
Fielding Consultancy **Limited's** accounts (*P*)
Tess's fear was apparent. (*P*)
Fernandes' restaurant (*the restaurant belonging to (Fernandes – names ending in an "iz" sound take an apostrophe but no extra "s"*) (*P*)
This **year's** calendar (*P*)
This **year's** events (*P*)
Past **years'** events (*P*) (*the events of past years*)
I need to give six **months'** notice. (*P*)
Sally's Gooseberry Jam (*P*)
Alice's Strawberry Jam (*P*)
The **boat's Simon's** [the boat's – (contraction of *boat is*) and Simon's – (possessive form of Simon, showing that the boat belongs to Simon) (*C, P*)
Young **People's** Services (*P*)
Thomas's room **isn't** at all tidy; **it's** a mess. (*P, C, C*)
This shop sells **children's** shoes. (*P*)

He is due to move up to Mrs **Morris's** class next year. (*P*)
Men's Captain (*P*)
Seniors' Captain (*P*)
Women's Captain (*P*)
Ladies' Captain (*P*)
Children's Captain (*P*)
Goat's meat (*P*)
Lamb's liver (*P*)
Susan's children's school is closing next year. (*P, P*)
It was his father **Bill's** car. (*P*)
The recipe is one of my mother **Anne's**. (*P*)
Jack is a friend of my **son's**. (*P*)
Millie was one of my daughter **Jane's** best friends. (*P*)
Mr and Mrs **James's daughter's dogs'** names are Tim and Sid (*P,P,P*)
Mr and Mrs **Fox's sons'** ages are 17 and 14 (*P,P*)
Tom's and Jerry's cartoon characters are brilliant (*P,P*)
Marion and Steve's house is a large extended bungalow (*P*)
She wrecked her husband **Alec's** car. (*P*)

The following are just as they are traditionally written:

- Mother's Day
- Father's Day
- Valentine's Day
- All Souls' Day

- St Patrick's Day
- April Fool's Day
- New Year's Day

And no apostrophe is needed in any of the following:

- CDs and DVDs (*not CD's and DVD's*)
- Hundreds of people
- The team played its best.
- Each of the divisions has its own recruitment policy.
- Everything is included in its plan.
- Please give me a demo to show me how the phone works.
- Shall we meet at the pub for lunch?
- One of our students fell ill on the morning of the exam.

12 – Explaining why the apostrophe is there

In this chapter I explain why the apostrophes are where they are in the correct examples that follow.

The film captures all the excitement of the young royals' nine-day tour.

The nine-day tour belongs to the young royals and, written in this way, *the young royals* needs an apostrophe to show that the nine-day tour belongs to them. The apostrophe is inserted after the "s" because there are two of them, that is, *royals* is a plural word. (See ch 1)

The film captures all the excitement of William and Kate's nine-day tour.

The nine-day tour belongs to William and Kate as a couple—they are treated as a single entity—which is why the apostrophe comes at the end of the couple's names. If there were several tours that William and Kate attended separately, then it would be written: "The film captures all the excitement of William's and Kate's tours". (See ch 7)

Michael's struggling to juggle his responsibilities.

In this example, the apostrophe is showing that there is a letter missing and two words have been contracted into one, ie *Michael is* struggling to juggle his responsibilities. (See ch 2)

Now it's time for the judges to vote.

Remember that an apostrophe in *its* means that it is either short for *it is* or *it has*. *Now it is time for the judges to vote*. (See ch 3)

It seems they're not being entirely honest.

The apostrophe here is showing that two words have been contracted into one and, if written in the longer form would be: *It seems they are not being entirely honest*. (See ch 2)

Within a few minutes' walk

This is saying: within a walk of a few minutes. When using the shortened form, minutes is then possessive and needs an apostrophe; the apostrophe goes after the "s" because *minutes* is a plural word. Other examples are: *in one day's time* or *in a few days' time*, ie time of one day or time of a few days. (See ch 1)

Fred is a friend of my father's

I apologise for this one, but this is a real anomaly and one that I don't understand the logic of myself. I would have expected that the correct way to write this would be *Fred is a friend of my father* but, having researched this extensively, it seems that this is the correct way to write it even though it appears to be a double negative. In its defence, we do say *Anne is a friend of mine* or *Stephen is a friend of his*, rather than *Anne is a friend of me* or *Stephen is a friend of him*. The way to avoid this is to say *Anne is my friend* and *Stephen is his friend*. But have you noticed the subtle difference in meaning? *Stephen is a friend of his* implies that Stephen is one of several of his friends, whereas *Stephen is his friend* does not imply the same meaning.

Consider this:

The recipe is one of my mother's, which is no doubt what we would say, but perhaps it is really a shortened way of saying, the recipe is one of my mother's recipes; this then makes sense.

Even though *Fred is a friend of my father's* is technically correct, it would appear that both *Fred is a friend of my father* and *Fred is a friend of my father's* are both accepted nowadays.

Appendix

(Actual apostrophe queries received and answers given since writing the first (e-book) edition of this book)

(Names have been changed where deemed appropriate.)

Q: *"All Year 11's are invited to a revision session". Please could you tell me whether year 11's has an apostrophe or not and the reasons why it does?*

A: This does not need an apostrophe because it is a straight plural. The only exception to this would be in a phrase such as, "Mind your p's and q's" because without the apostrophes it wouldn't make sense to the reader ie, "Mind your ps and qs". If you were to write, "Mind your Ps and Qs" then the meaning is clear and it should not have apostrophes. In your sentence, an apostrophe would be incorrect. The correct version is:
"All Year 11s are invited to a revision session."

Q: *When referring to multiple beneficiaries I understand that the singular "beneficiary" changes to "beneficiaries" but, if something belongs to those beneficiaries is an apostrophe required? For example "The best way to meet the beneficiaries needs..."*

A: The correct way to write this is "The best way to meet the beneficiaries' needs".

This is a shortened way of saying – "the needs of the beneficiaries". To make this plural word ie, beneficiaries, possessive you need to add just an apostrophe at the end because the word already ends in an "s". If the plural word did not end in an "s" eg, children, people, men, women, then these words would need an apostrophe in addition to an "s" to make them possessive ie, children's, people's, men's, women's. These words are treated as if they were singular words.

Q: *Parents views and childrens views?*

A: The plural of parent is parents and therefore the apostrophe goes after the "s" ie, parents' views – assuming that you are referring to the views of more than one parent. If, however, you are referring to the views of one parent, it would be parent's views, which normally would be preceded by "the" or "a".

The plural of child is children, without the "s", and therefore the apostrophe goes before the "s" ie, children's views.

So, when a plural ends in an "s", just add an apostrophe. When a plural does not end in an "s" ie, children, women, men, people, then you need to add an apostrophe and an "s" eg, women's, men's, people's.

Q: *I'm unsure of the apostrophe after the word girls in these sentences (the girls haven't done their homework) and (close the door of the girls cloakroom) is it girls'?*

A: In the first sentence – the girls haven't done their homework – the word "girls" is simply a plural and not possessive. It's the same as saying, for example, I haven't done my homework or they haven't done their homework. The word "girls" in this instance should not have an apostrophe.

In your second sentence – close the door of the girls cloakroom – "girls" in this instance is possessive and should have an apostrophe. It is the shortened way of saying, "close the door of the cloakroom of the girls. To make the word "girls" possessive, you should ask, "who does the cloakroom belong to?" The answer is "the girls"; the apostrophe goes immediately after the word that is the answer to that question ie, girls. If the cloakroom were referring to only one girl, then it would be "close the door of the girl's cloakroom".

Q: *(Writings difficult for some people) and (Buy your cucumber and lettuces here) - also whether they are omissions or possessions.*

A: "Writings difficult for some people" is a short way of saying "writing is difficult for some people". "Writings" is a contraction ie, where two words have been merged into one ie, "writing" and "is". Therefore, in the word "writings", the letter "i" is missing and it needs an apostrophe to show that a letter has been omitted. The correct way to write this is "writing's difficult for some people".

In the second sentence – buy your cucumber and lettuces here – the word lettuces is just a plural and is not possessive. Straight plurals ie, more than one of something, never have an apostrophe - an apostrophe should not be added to make something into a plural. The plural of lettuce is lettuces, and the plural of cucumber is cucumbers.

Q: *A current child care business operates under the name "A N Other Centre for Children". We are about to open a second premises and wish to change the business name to indicate the fact that there is more than one centre, i.e "A N Other Centres for Children", however there is some confusion as to whether an apostrophe is required after the s in centres or not.*

A: In this phrase, the word "Centres" is simply a plural and straight plurals do not need an apostrophe; in fact, to insert one would be incorrect. So, the correct way to write the name is: "A N Other Centres for Children" without an apostrophe. You would only need an apostrophe in the word "centres" if it were possessive.

Q: *learners development; the Academys behaviour policy - where do the apostrophes go for the words learners and academy?*

A: The first phrase depends on whether you are referring to just one or more than one learner. If you mean one learner, then the correct phrase is "learner's development", but if you mean more than one learner then it should be "learners' development". With a singular word, the apostrophe goes before the "s", and with a plural word it goes after the "s".

The second phrase is straightforward ie, "the Academy's behaviour policy" – the behaviour policy of the Academy. Again, as it is just one Academy then the apostrophe goes before the "s".

Q: *My order of preference is identical to Will's. I think this is correct, but does Will own his order of preference?*

A: Your sentence is really a short form of saying, "My order of preference is identical to Will's order of preference."

The clue to the answer to your question is in the "My order of preference" phrase, in that you own your order of preference simply denoted by the word "my". In the same way, Will owns his order of preference too and therefore the word Will's is possessive and is correct as you've written it.

Q: *Each party's commitments or each parties commitments? (there are 5 parties)*

A: The correct version is "Each party's commitments", even though there are 5 parties.

The word "each" is only used with one of something and in using the word "each" you are distinguishing between the commitments of the individual parties. Were you to say, for example, "the parties' commitments" (meaning the commitments of all the parties) then, as shown, the apostrophe would come after the "s" of "parties".

Q: *"...am I using correctly the apostrophe s in the following sentence?: 'supporting our communities' well being."*

A: If you are talking about more than one community, then your sentence is absolutely correct. However, if you were referring to just one community then the sentence would be "supporting our community's well-being".

Q: *Should it be:-*
(A) teacher's desk or
(B) teachers' desk

A: I am assuming the desk belongs to just one teacher. If this is correct, then it is (A) teacher's desk. If, however, the desk belongs to more than one teacher it would be (B) teachers' desk. The apostrophe comes before the "s" if you're referring to only one of something, and after the "s" when there's more than one.

Q: *Does this sentence need an apostrophe? "Time to order next years planner".*

A: This is really a shortened way of saying, "Time to order your planner for/of next year" and in the shortened form "next year" becomes possessive and therefore needs an apostrophe. As "next year" is singular, the apostrophe goes before the "s". The correct form is therefore "Time to order next year's planner".

Q: *Where to place the apostrophe in the following sentence? "A N Other won the viewers choice award."*

A: The award is the choice of the viewers, which means that the choice belongs to the viewers, making it possessive. Also, because there is more than one viewer, the apostrophe goes after the "s". The correct way to write this is: A N Other won the viewers' choice award.

Q: *Compiling a club Management Committee list. Mens Captain - where does apostrophe go? And do I need one for Ladies Captain?*

A: The correct way to write these is:

Men's Captain
Ladies' Captain

Regarding the men - ask yourself, who does the Captain belong or refer to? The answer is "the men" – the apostrophe goes immediately after whatever word is the answer to that question. Regarding the ladies - who does the Captain belong or refer to? The answer is "the ladies" – the apostrophe goes after whatever word is the answer to that question.

When a plural eg, "men" doesn't end in an "s", then you add an apostrophe followed by an "s". When a plural eg, "ladies" ends in an "s", you only need to add an apostrophe and no further "s".

Incidentally, were it to be women, instead of ladies, then it would be Women's Captain.

One more tip: try turning the phrase around to its longest form ie, Captain of the Men, Captain of the Ladies. Again the apostrophe goes after the word "Men" and after the word "Ladies".

Q: *Can you please advise me as to where the apostrophe (if any!) goes when I want to write 'merry christmas Olivers' meaning merry christmas to the Oliver's family! Is it just a plural?*

A: This is just a plural and "Merry Christmas Olivers" is entirely correct; there is no requirement for an apostrophe. I assume you are talking about the Olivers as a family, with the surname of Oliver. (Just as an aside – it would be "Merry Christmas to the Oliver family" rather than Oliver's family.)

Q: *What about when you are referring to parties. For example, the parties rights and conditions. Will it be the parties' rights and conditions?*

A: Yes, you are absolutely right – it would be "the parties' rights and conditions" because it's the rights and conditions of the parties.

Q: *I bought a cushion for friends stating "Christmas at the Kerr's" is this not correct?*

A: I will assume that the friends' surname is Kerr. The house belongs to the Kerrs (the plural of Kerr), which means it is the Kerrs' house.

When you say Christmas at the Kerrs' you are really saying Christmas at the Kerrs' house or home, but leaving off the word house/home. The correct way to write it is: Christmas at the Kerrs'.

Q: *Where does the apostrophe go in the following: Mens hat and Mans hat*

A: I think this one confuses many people, but ask yourself "who does the hat belong to?". The answers are:

men
man

The apostrophe goes immediately after whatever the answer to the question is; so it's men's hat and man's hat. Men, women and children are all treated in the same way ie, as if they were singular, rather than plural words, because they do not end in an "s". For example: men's shoes, women's clothing, children's books.

Answers to quizzes

Answers to introductory apostrophe quiz

1b) The people's vote
(Chs 1 and 4)

2a) Is this mine or yours?
(Ch 10)

3a) The man, whose car I crashed into, is my neighbour
(Ch 9)

4b) Jack is a friend of my mother's
(Ch 12)

5b) The boys were told the sweets were all theirs
(Chs 6 and 10)

6b) Two weeks' notice
(Ch 1)

7a) The men's wives went with them on the trip
(Chs 1 and 4)

8b) Where are the women's toilets?
(Chs 1 and 4)

9b) Who told you it's yours?
(Ch 3)

10a) Who's that man?
(Ch 9)

11a) Mr and Mrs Smith's house was burgled
(Ch 7)

12a) The Smiths' house is in darkness
(Ch 7)

13a) MOTs carried out here
(Chs 6 and 11)

14a) Whose bag is this?
(Ch 9)

15b) Mind your Ps and Qs
(Ch 6)

16a) The salad contained lettuces and tomatoes
(Ch 6)

17b) Which shoes? The red or the white ones?
(Ch 6)

18b) You're late!
(Ch 2)

19b) The dog has injured its paw
(Ch 3)

20a) Shall we go to the children's playground?
(Chs 1 and 4)

21a) I've been invited to Sue and Mark's wedding
(Chs 7 and 11)

22a) Don't forget your phone
(Ch 2)

23a) She was born in the '20s
(Ch 2)

24b) He was born in the 1920s
(Ch 2)

25a) Look where you're going!
(Ch 2)

26a) The rain's stopped
(Ch 2)

27a) Policemen's helmets
(Chs 1 and 4)

28a) Tell me it's not going to rain
(Ch 3)

29a) The company has expanded its product portfolio
(Ch 3)

30a) Women's shoes are next to the ladies' handbags
(Ch 4)

Answers to Its or It's quiz

1 a) It's time to go! *(It is time to go!)*

2 a) The dog's eaten its lunch

(The dog has eaten its lunch)

3 b) Let's not forget that it's only been a year

(Let us not forget that it has only been a year)

4 d) It's my job to safeguard its location

(It is my job to safeguard its location)

5 a) The project team achieved all of its deliverables

6 a) Unfortunately it's been taken out of my hands

(Unfortunately it has been taken out of my hands)

7 b) If it's genuine, where's its label?

(If it is genuine, where is its label?)

8 a) It's already been useful; it's worth its weight in gold

(It has already been useful; it is worth its weight in gold)

9 c) Poor baby - it's crying because it's dropped its teddy bear

(Poor baby – it is crying because it has dropped its teddy bear)

A final note

I sincerely hope that you find the answers to your apostrophe queries in this book – if not, please feel free to email your particular question to sfielding@commasense.co.uk and I will try to respond within a few hours. Then, once I've amassed another pile of queries, I'll write a third edition to update the contents of this book.

Glossary

Abbreviation
shortened form of a word, eg phone

Adjective
a word used to describe someone or something, eg small

Contraction
Where two words have been merged into one, eg can't, haven't

Plural
The form of the word meaning more than one, eg women, socks

Possessive
Is an adjective indicating possession as in "the possessive form of a word"

Singular
The form of the word meaning one of it, eg woman, sock

Bibliography

R L Trask, *The Penguin Guide to Punctuation*, Penguin Books, 1997

Lynne Truss, *Eats Shoots & Leaves*, Profile Books, 2003

Debra Hart May, *Proofreading Plain & Simple*, Career Press, 1997

E S C Weiner and Andrew Delahunty, *The Oxford Guide to English Usage*, Oxford University Press, 1994

Philip Gooden, *Who's Whose?* A & C Black Publishing Ltd, 2004

Caroline Taggart and J A Wines, *My Grammar and I*, Michael O'Mara Books Limited, 2011

Annette Lyon, *There, Their, They're,* Createspace, 2009

This book hopefully answers the apostrophe questions that you're unable to find the answers to elsewhere.

25437844R00052

Printed in Great Britain
by Amazon